Enormous Morning

ALSO BY PHILIP SCHULTZ

POETRY

Luxury
The Wherewithal
The God of Loneliness: Selected and New Poems
Failure
Living in the Past
The Holy Worm of Praise
My Guardian Angel Stein
Deep Within the Ravine
Like Wings

MEMOIR

Comforts of the Abyss
My Dyslexia

AS EDITOR

The Pushcart Book of 21st Century Poetry and Prose
(Philip Schultz and Bill Henderson, coeditors)

Enormous Morning

Poems

Philip Schultz

W. W. NORTON & COMPANY

Independent Publishers Since 1923

Copyright © 2026 by Philip Schultz

All rights reserved
Printed in the United States of America
First Edition

For information about permission to reproduce selections from
this book, write to Permissions, W. W. Norton & Company, Inc.,
500 Fifth Avenue, New York, NY 10110

For information about special discounts for bulk purchases, please
contact W. W. Norton Special Sales at specialsales@wwnorton.com or
800-233-4830

Manufacturing by Versa Press
Book design by Brooke Koven
Production manager: Ramona Wilkes

Library of Congress Control Number: 2025942596

ISBN 978-1-324-12382-8

W. W. Norton & Company, Inc., 500 Fifth Avenue, New York, NY 10110
www.wwnorton.com

W. W. Norton & Company Ltd., 15 Carlisle Street, London W1D 3BS

Authorized EU representative: EAS, Mustamäe tee 50, 10621 Tallinn, Estonia

1 2 3 4 5 6 7 8 9 0

For Monica

*Now before is left behind and morning
begins always for the first time*

Enormous morning, ponderous, meticulous;
gray light streaking each bare branch

—ELIZABETH BISHOP, "FIVE FLIGHTS UP"

CONTENTS

Enormous Morning	1
Flesh	3
Sacrifice	4
Navalny	5
Suffering	6
The Big Story and the Little Story	8
The Present Moment	10
Happing Endings	12
Good News	13
For the Time Being	15
Crazy	17
In the Time of Corona	19
Broken Hallelujah: After Eric Fischl	20
Spoiled Prayers	21
School Buses	22
The Art of Wailing	24
Somewhere North of Extinction	26
On the Edge of Things	28

Isabelle at Morandi	29
Just Down the Street	30
Sigmund's Equation	31
Santos	32
My Neighbor Ed	34
Ode to The East Hampton Star	36
A Marriage Song	38
Women Rabbis	39
Our Story	40
For Eli on His Twenty-Fifth Birthday	41
What Comes Next	42
Penelope	44
The Designer	45
The Middle	47
Early and Late	49
My Mistakes	50
Blame	52
My Heart	54
Democracy	56
Something and Nothing	58
Acknowledgments	*81*

Enormous Morning

Enormous Morning

It's an early winter morning,
the morning of my 80th year,
and I'm walking my Great Pyrenees mix, Binx,
through the Cedar Lawn Cemetery,
visiting the Grimshaws, Talmages and Kings,
whose opinions are echoing off
their mildewed limestone and slate names:
Benny Janes in 1706 still wondering
if a second windmill on Old Hook Hill
will improve the value of his estate,
young William Lamb arguing with old Henry Hadel
about the odds for and against going to WWI
or debtors' prison, Lucy Reutershan advising
Sally Ann Bennet against wearing a handsewn
wedding dress, it's not fine or lacy enough,
and a Jeffrey Arnold Cobb IV, wondering where
on Shelter Island to properly bury slaves,
while yellow-breasted warblers caw at us
about graves we've left untended, blessings
squandered. And yes, here I am,
older than I ever imagined I'd be,
wedged between the living and dead,
singing spoiled prayers, wondering why
I still want to reach across all the sorrow
and make my father understand that forgiveness
isn't absolution or mercy, but the grace
that love makes, the only true wealth.

And here we all are, children hurrying off to school,
holding Mother's hand, heads held high,
shoulders straight, an enormous morning opening
wide its pearly jade wings over everything
beginning again from the beginning.

Flesh

speaks by blushing,
wrinkling, graying
with age and grief,
remembers each caress
and what was felt
for those who gave it.
Sly, clairvoyant, and wise
beyond its ecology,
it never reminds us
it is sacred, that its beauty
is born of woman,
knows resilience
is its strength,
that it can be flayed,
blown apart, drained
of its mother's breath,
every ounce of youth
and dignity, made to forget
it is living tissue,
and even then,
the memory of its genius
continues
in each precious touch.
I swear to you it continues.

Sacrifice

After my sister was stillborn, Mother
was told it was dangerous to try again,
but she did, happily. After Father died,
she told me stories about how, one week
before their wedding, he lost everything
and asked to move into her mother's house
for a few months, and stayed twenty years;
how, when her teachers came to her house
to plead for her orthodox father to let her stay
in school, she was brilliant, wrote like an angel,
he sent them away, education, he said, was wasted
on girls. Half her life a filing clerk, the other half
counting coins from my father's vending machines,
disappointment the salt she soaked her feet in each night.
At her Alzheimer's ward, she showed me a big black book
in which she kept every scrap of my existence sealed
in plastic. I was the one thing she did right, she said.
Lillian, Lilith her namesake, the first woman on earth,
before Eve, exiled for believing she was Adam's equal,
from which the word the idea lullaby derives, like the ones
she sang to me at night about being strong and good,
surviving the bitterness that lives in us like bad dreams.
Sometimes I walk the house at night the way she did,
looking for the strength to undo all the hurt and shame,
be a little more of what she so gladly sacrificed everything for.

Navalny

Sacrifice is an expensive word,
an even more expensive idea.
Imagine the cost of giving up everything
for one's belief, loving your ideals more than yourself,
surviving every kind of abuse, day after day,
the expense of such passion, such faith.
Where does such strength of will,
belief in the idea of goodness come from?
Did Alexei A. Navalny wish to mentor the world,
set an example history couldn't repudiate?
Imagine the pride and satisfaction, the cunning,
the delight and torment in destroying before the eyes
of the world the conscience of his tormentors.
Now it's our turn. Now we must summon
the courage to at least ask what we would sacrifice,
whether we deserve, can afford our freedom.

Suffering

Hiding doesn't help,
it will find you anywhere,
remind you of your every
unpardonable act and word,
every attempt to undermine its authority.
Fear is its currency, distrust and blame its strengths.
Seldom is it personal, or original,
never bankrupt of ideas on how to prevail,
and yes, it has benefits: helping us distinguish
between mere misery and abject wretchedness.
And of course, it can be performed anywhere,
in any position, while driving, clipping toenails,
strolling absentmindedly down the corridors
of common sense. Its intelligence and devotion to detail,
inexhaustible. Its abhorrence to good news,
every flavor of sympathy, fondness of isolation
are renown. Free yourself of longing, it pleads,
any notion of triumph, strive after the unattainable,
make a shrine of desire and instinct, just sit there
listening to your anxieties resonate into a symphony
of betrayals, forgive and believe in nothing
but the opacity of boredom and endless change.
A sanctuary for self-pity, repository for shame
of every denomination, it's your last loyal friend,

it croons in your dreams, give in, deny, postpone,
remain unadorned, invisible and divided, forgive
and believe in nothing but boredom and endless change,
forage interminably in its magnanimous garden
of blindness and rage.

The Big Story and the Little Story

The Little Story is quite little, about
the size of your house and street,
fixates on bank accounts, toothpaste,
clean underwear and what's behind
the grins of neighbors and friends.
The Big Story obsesses about what things
mean, the day after tomorrow, why something
is or isn't extravagant enough to satisfy
its ambitions. The Little Story enjoys
being taken for granted, misunderstood,
and misplaced. Too often, it forgets what
its many grudges and mistakes were about,
not to mention, all its conceits. The Big Story
wants to be feared, indulged, and thoroughly
respected, if not believed. Which is why
it names its episodes: Reality, History, Politics
and Missed Opportunities. The Little Story
likes to complain to strangers at bus stops
about its job, wife and kids, how it's constantly
being smothered by ungrateful subtleties.
The Big Story relishes resumes, privileges,
and everything ever said or thought about fate.
The Little Story abhors sour endings, its own
ludicrous schemes, being left behind and forgotten.
The Big Story worries about being big enough,
especially late at night when its conscience
wants to sleep. The Little Story mainly fears

being swallowed by the Big Story, which fears
only itself. Each agree on one thing: why the Tao
asks us to think of the small as large, the few as many,
and what it means by practicing eternity
while being stuck somewhere in between.

The Present Moment

> *Life was never anything more than a present moment*
> *always vanishing*
> —ARTHUR SCHOPENHAUER

Yes, an anxious, impulsive, aloof, slippery fish,
always worrying about being understood,
visible, and hospitable enough,
which is why perhaps it's seldom docile enough
to entertain even casual visitors
in its moody, inapt grasp
and can't bear to hold onto anything,
is always dropping things.
I'm its prisoner, it insists,
a refugee forever begging the future to rescue me.
Is this why it's always angry at me
and refuses to forgive something I said or thought?
Don't pretend you don't know who's speaking to you,
it whispers in my dreams, I'm the poet, not you,
the reason everything you write is irreverent,
tenuous, riddled with duplicitous ambiguities,
that you're ignorant of the difference between triumph and praise.
Yes, I'm where all your courage, fears,
and intuitions are hidden, the reason reality
so often feels like a vortex of ravenous schemes.
Please, it groans, stop pleading for attention,
a little kindness, an occasional hug,
nothing else can save you,

for just one moment be irritable, frivolous, insatiable,
embrace all your misgivings,
bid farewell to all your disguises,
the wrath of your blessings,
be wrong every other Wednesday,
unfasten the hair shirt of your sacrilege,
honor all your petty details,
appease your terrors and anxieties,
be spiteful, please,
just this one time,
embrace each epic yearning,
rhyme.

Happy Endings

Recently, my wife and I were enjoying
a movie about a happy marriage
when it suddenly soured into a caterwaul
of grievance, and then a noisy novel
I was relishing also promised happiness
before abruptly divorcing itself
from any semblance of reality.
Yes, reality is hard work, and,
like us, is often tired and just wants
to be left alone. Happy endings
are rarely reasonable, after all,
they must work hard to earn our belief
and faith, and often, like us, too,
are prisoners of their premonitions
and misgivings. I'm not asking for rapture,
just a moment or two of merriment,
an intimation of well-being. And yes,
nervous, insatiable, our blessings
are seldom confident of our sincerity.
They too require encouragement
in preparing for the unimaginable.
Be patient, hopeful, I remind myself,
happiness arrives when least expected,
almost always uninvited. No matter how
unprepared we are the inexorable
eventually knocks. In fact, there it is now,
out on the lawn, lulling about, waiting
for an ending happy enough to be invited inside.

Good News

Embedded in my late-night community of insomniacs,
here I am again, seeking diversion from wildfires,
school shootings and bombed hospitals,
watching an old movie called *Good News*
about a football hero falling in love
with his French tutor. Made in 1947,
after endless war, it's trying valiantly to point
a way forward. Unlike me, these happy lovers
aren't older than their imaginations, dealing
with all sorts of stubborn maladies. Indeed,
everyone here is young and swinging
everyone else around a glittering dance floor,
ecstatic about what lies ahead. Without doubt,
the younger me would now be hopping over sofas,
celebrating each precious moment of sanity.
Yes, we're all relieved when bad news is happening
elsewhere to someone else, at least for the time being.
A week ago, wearing a cap and gown,
my youngest son skied down a Vermont hill,
happily embracing his future, while two weeks before
the wing of a plane his best friend's father
was in broke off and the future also drowned.
Plato believed we live in a restless state
of *continual Becoming and never Being.*
Yes, the machinery of our endless striving
after something that forever evades us,
the closest we come to happiness perhaps.
In any case, here I am again, embedded in

the wellsprings of mystery, seeking
the smallest scrap of certainty,
whatever remains buoyant and unbroken,
racing toward the bottom of an expectant hill
where the forever changing and irreversible future
waits patiently, for the time being.

For the Time Being

Long before I understood
what Hegel meant by
a "highway of despair,"
or knew or cared who he was,
far down inside somewhere
I understood that most of those
tobacco-spitting-quick-to-be-enraged
TV cowboys and gangsters
would all one day be dead,
not just pretending, but gone,
buried, done with. That my always-
obsessed-with-success father
and radiantly devoted mother
and forever-praying-to-a-God-
ignorant-of-her grandma, along
with everybody downstairs
and us kids up in the balcony
every Saturday morning would
one day be nowhere to be found,
along with everyone in Mr. Bein's
big red bus and the never-smiling
blue-rinse cashier at Freddy's Ice Cream
and just about every squeaky-clean-
brassier-and-raincoat-trying-on
customer in Sibley's Department Store
and even the sour fluorescence
we all sat under at school would
one day become part of Hegel's

arcane highway stretching all the way
to this August Sunday morning
in which my wife and two sons
are happily asleep upstairs while
I'm sitting here in my study, watching
these curious filaments of thought
filter through the dusty pink light,
for the time being.

Crazy

> *I believe that the torturer is as depraved by his acts as the one who is tortured . . .*
> —BREYTEN BREYTENBACH

Last night my wife came downstairs to ask
if I was throwing a dinner party. Alone,
I was arguing with something someone said
twenty years ago, finally, responding brilliantly.
Recently, I stopped biting my nails, but still pick
at my fingers, follow the beloved faces
of my favorite dead for blocks on end.
Everyone in my family kept secrets from themselves,
such as why they all slapped themselves, repeatedly.
Uncle Jake stood at the toilet mirror, daring himself
to try it again. Grandma once slapped Mrs. Tillem
at Levy's deli because, she cursed, God told her to.
Father slapped mostly his fate. We all talked to ourselves
so loudly no one ever heard anything anyone else ever said.
Asked why he used irony to describe a death camp,
Tadeusz Borowski said: a defense against intolerable pain,
an admission of failure. Because reality was a necessary illusion?
Once, over dinner, a friend described the indignities
done to him and others by those of his God and race;
how each night in solitary confinement there was no air to breathe,
nothing to grasp, distort, resist. For years, day after day,
he walked inside his tiny cell, chanting the names of the dead.
Why hadn't he gone crazy, I asked. Staring into the darkness

of my being, he said, "What makes you think I didn't?"
What's dark in my nature is also devious. At night,
in the quiet of my cell, I practice the art of solace,
irony, and catharsis. Condone and forgive nothing,
the past reminds me, not even the obscenity of truth,
always a last slap in the face.

In the Time of Corona

Our mailman, Joe, always stopped to talk
about Bernie, being vegan, and baseball.
When our dog, Penelope, died,
he told me he wished he'd let her bite him
just once, a kind of goodbye.
Now, under his mask, only his eyes are alive,
he barely nods, and hurries by.
Small talk is what my wife misses most.
It's what a small town runs on, she thinks,
that and everyday catastrophes.
The one we live in is near the ocean,
where everyone goes to feel illustrious and justified.
The rich weekenders live here now,
and, apparently, own the sky.
Their helicopters hover above like conspiracy theories.
Our lovely neighbor, after learning
she had lymphoma, thought, at least now
she could hug someone. Upstairs,
our 21-year-old son is quarantined with his girlfriend.
He got it after his college closed and the nurse
who tested me said not to write a will just yet.
Suddenly, even melancholy is a symptom,
a kind of goodbye, and everyone is a Nostradamus,
hiding behind their eyes, speaking in cryptograms
and sighs only they understand.

Broken Hallelujah: After Eric Fischl

Here he is: the artist as combatant, alone inside
the darkness of his arena, his eye scalding
our imaginations, daring us to enter the fever
of revelation, the violence of vision. His hands
anointed red, resting between rounds of agony
and satisfaction, waiting for the exaltation to begin.
The blackness of his clothes sweeping us ever deeper
into the frenzy of inspiration, the unforeseen. Seated
beside him, Tumbling Woman, struggling to take flight,
rise above being calamity's mistress, the ransom of history.
The tools: easels, paper towels, color, canvas imploding
into the nakedness of adoration, April in Paris, afire in light,
the woman standing behind him, swallowing her testimony,
staring at the man imprisoned inside her story. Yes, paintings
inside paintings, the formulas of passion bloodied but unbroken,
stretched across millenniums of crawling forever deeper
into jubilation, the mortal core rendered visible, vulnerable.
Yes, there, hidden deep inside his gaze: us, pleading for meaning,
to be understood, forgiven for wanting to be touched by fate,
and saved, yes, saved.

Spoiled Prayers

> *All that is mine I carry with me*
> —CICERO QUOTING BIAS OF PRIENE,
> ONE OF THE SEVEN SAGES OF GREECE

Yes, all that is mine, everything I own and disown,
see and forget, all my mistakes, shames and rewards,
everything exalting, feckless and disillusioning, promises
kept and disavowed, the junkyard behind our old house,
its gurgling toilets, rusty razor blades, hills of grinding engines
and rampaging rats, smells constantly refreshed, yes,
everything buried in memory's graveyard, I carry with me:
Alzheimer's singing lullabies off-key in Mother's mouth,
her eyes empty of me, the fireworks high over Lake Ontario
every Fourth of July, the prosperity that never arrived,
the old Polish woman screaming at fate on the always late
Joseph Avenue bus, the staticky newsreels cataloguing
stolen Jewish diaries, paintings, and scrolls piled high
in the basilica of my dreams, where it's always 1945 and there,
high on the domed ceiling, a choir of orphaned angels singing
requiems off-key, grieving forsaken keepsakes too heavy
to be carried all the way to revelation, yes, please, look up
and hear mercy's retinue, where, hidden deep inside boxes
and crates, spoiled prayers plead to be believed, and freed . . .

School Buses

> *When walking, I am asleep, when sleeping, I dream reality.*
> —CZESLAW MILOSZ

It's Daylight Savings time
and a two-hour snow delay
it's raining three mornings straight
and the sun is hiding behind Lucy's bangs—and
there they are—the yellowtail whippoorwills
trembling to a stop looping around corners
bursting with curious brilliantly bored squinty faces
pressed against snow-dusted rain-streaked sun-bleached windows
stained with laughter toothpaste applesauce last-ditch schemes
to redeem self-esteem—always almost on time
coughing belching cantankerous fleets stopping
only to start before a lowering train guard
paroxysms of flashing red lights dancing down
jumping jack hills loopy byways cul-de-sacs racing
reflections of geese across the pond carrying
native-to-nowhere feelings opinions temper tantrums
screeching sideways past One Stop Deli Pepperoni Pizza
St. Luke's always about-to-topple steeple
raccoons squirrels deer squashed on Cedar Street
by what Uncle Hank calls fate (his red Chevy pickup)
swinging pigtails plastic spoons beating three-fourth time
on the backs of seats heads—all the zipping up unbuttoning
hiccupping sneezing thumb-strumming growth spurts

Henrietta the divine calling Fat Sammy a *dreampie*
as Latin 2 homework airplanes circumnavigate
the tumultuous stratosphere of All Saints' Eve (Halloween)
everything always on the verge of becoming astonishing—all that
sweet hunger for one last smile from dear Miss Crittenden
crying at the blackboard because it's her birthday and no one
remembers anything about the Peloponnesian Wars
who wrote the Declaration of Independence—Miss Crittenden
who foresaw what would become of all our longing for the holes
time leaves after it takes back everything it gave—Miss Crittenden
who took my hand and led me across the world of Clinton Avenue
to the me now sitting here at my desk wondering what became
of all those busy brilliant heroic daydreams until 3PM
when the accordion doors opened on all our mothers aunts older sisters
and grandmothers waiting maybe since the Peloponnesian Wars
to welcome us back into the whirling jubilant unwieldly splendor
of their arms—Lord!

The Art of Wailing

He who shows himself is not conspicuous.
The way is for ever nameless.

—LAO TZU

Jim, older than me, and,
apparently, clumsier,
is swearing as he bangs my stretcher
against the back of the ambulance.
Billy, the young driver, laughs
as he gently slides me inside,
where Betsy, a retired librarian my sons loved,
recalls hearing me read a poem
about pumpernickel that made her hungry.
"Let her," Jim says, "and she'll talk you to death."
"Well," she says, "you failed a few tests,
no big thing, a stent or two, relax."
Now we're running traffic lights,
the wailing reaching all the way to high C.
"You'll get fentanyl," she sings, "might be inspiring."
"Well, if he writes one, you'll be in it," he sighs.
"Your wife's sculpture is at the Nature Conservancy,"
she adds, "where I also volunteer."
"Yes, well, I help out at three firehouses," he shouts,
"don't get me started." I volunteer for nothing,
my charity, remembering everything.
"I love poetry," she sighs, "but it gives me headaches."
"Hang in there, fella," Jim winks, "we're almost there."

Outside the back window, a flock of pink clouds spell out
a line by Lao Tzu: *Governing a large state is like boiling a small fish.*
Yes, if abused, both stink. Now the wailing's inside and out,
a medley of Dylan's rasping loneliness, Monk's joyous reckonings,
Elvis rocking my jailhouse loose of all my precious bitterness—O life
please forgive my stumbling back-alley escapes into respectability,
my endless cacophony of unleavened regret and longing—please
one hour more of my wife and sons, glorious absurdity,
Gerard Manley Hopkins and making tragic mistakes,
my being my own favorite pursuit—O thank you thank you
for this beautiful nameless ungovernable stinky small pink fish . . .

Somewhere North of Extinction

Well, here we are again,
on our treadmills,
deep within a hospital's cardiac center,
two fellow rehabbers,
accountants I believe,
on either side of me,
watching Fox News while discussing
tax-free Caribbean vacations,
organized, I imagine, by Dante.
My silence, I assume they assume,
implies equal pleasure in seeing
noisy ideas being crucified.
My TV, tuned to the History Channel
by a previous tenant, shows
a jubilant Darwin wandering curiously
among incurious tortoises,
who, apparently, have no idea
what being naturally selected means,
other than, perhaps, having somehow adapted
to their new and surprising
personalities. In any case,
the surrounding clamor is triumphant,
we're all still here, after all,
on the treadmill of evolution,
somewhere north of extinction,

sweating happily, contemplating
our complex, peculiar strivings
toward the rewards of indefatigability,
one dogged assumption, cranky idea,
and tax-free holiday at a time.

On the Edge of Things

In Memory of Connie Fox

Yesterday, Monica and I said goodbye
to a painter friend in hospice, a wonderful woman
in her late nineties, who first came out here to the far
eastern edge of Long Island in 1979 with her
expressionist friend, Elaine de Kooning, whose husband,
Willem, rode his bicycle past her house every morning,
calling, "Good morning, Connie, best of luck!"
where she met her husband, the sculptor, Bill King,
each obsessed with ripping the unspoken out of the known,
the astonishing out of the everyday, the symphonic out
of each trembling breath. Having suffered a stroke,
she could now speak only in song, and with her daughter Megan
we all held hands and sang "I've Been Working on the Railroad,"
a song she sang to Megan as a girl. After kissing her goodbye,
my wife and I walked along the ocean, under the same red umbrella
she opened in her paintings, and I wished I could've thanked her
one last time for all those afternoons in her studio, revelation
dancing from floor to skylight, color trembling inside
whirling squares and sumptuous rectangles, her playing the fiddle
and Bill the piano at our sons' birthdays, her echoing laughter—yes,
thanked her for introducing me to myself, the man hidden inside
his own hours of light and ecstatic wings, thanked her for her gift
of passion for what lives on the edge of things. Yes, now paradise
will be seen the way it was meant to, one edgy red umbrella at a time.

Isabelle at Morandi

In Memory of Isabelle Deconinck

Yes, it's Wednesday morning and here you are,
at our café, Morandi, conducting 7th Avenue traffic
with breadsticks, the pigeons dancing outside
our window to the beat of your melodic stories.
You, a girl wandering the vibrant streets of Paris,
studying the viola in Oklahoma, of all places,
reviving the mysteries of the Belgian Congo,
each an ardent appetite pleading with me,
your teacher, to help you find the wonder
that permits the inner life to speak. Then,
one Wednesday, a story of chemo, radiation,
the infinite infusions of the lymphoma that took you
and your love, Davida, to the far side of imagination.
Every Wednesday another story of impossible striving,
and then, one morning, you grasped my hand and,
staring into my eyes, smiled brilliantly, as if having
finally seen the you you believed only I knew.
And yes, your last email, "I'm sick in a way
I never was before . . . lost 15 pounds in a week . . .
can barely stay in my body . . . I will always love
and support you . . ." And now, this Wednesday morning,
here you are, again, conducting all heaven's traffic
with your brilliant eyes, one more time.

Just Down the Street

Monica and I were walking to town
with our dog, Binx, when our kindly neighbor,
Doris, rushed over to us from her house
across the street. She'd just been diagnosed
with lymphoma, she said, and would start chemo
treatments next week. Her nurse, standing
in her driveway, waved. We know her well enough
to say hello, smile when passing. Once my wife
and I helped her find her lost dog, for which
she's thanked us repeatedly. Now her large
quiet blue eyes look frozen with, what—disbelief?
Struggling with words, perhaps she's hoping
we can tell her what to think and feel. Despite
the pandemic, we all hug, and she cries, won't
let go of our hands. She has our phone numbers,
we say, call if there's anything we can do. Then,
continuing our journey, once again it's a beautiful
Tuesday afternoon in early fall, the elms, maples
and sycamores lush with expectation. Their silence
feels earned, a source of profound comfort and faith.
Yes, here we are again, alone together, improvising
answers to questions waiting just down the street.

Sigmund's Equation

Before anyone knew what a computer was,
my wife's uncle Sigmund created a formula
for New York City's first mainline computer,
using what he said was a single variable equation,
$-10X = X - 10$, a formula, he said, that somehow
makes everything equal. When in doubt, he said,
"Just multiply everything by 10, even your height,
age or desires, they all work out." Being bad at math,
I didn't understand but believed him. Sigmund
spent his childhood in a labor camp in Siberia,
a slave to fanaticism. By the time he was fifteen
the end had been ripped out of his every beginning,
the beginning starved to death. Math was his way
of imagining the miracle of his imagination, I believe.
Last Sunday, we buried him in Queens, my wife, me,
an orthodox rabbi, and several angels hovering
uneasily overhead. Angels aren't respected as much
as they used to be, one whispered. They came because
Sigmund is famous for inspiring God to multiply
redemption beyond even its capacity for jubilation.
One hundred feet away several Hasidic mourners
were loudly singing prayers for a deaf God to hear.
Sigmund, also hard of hearing, will hear our prayers
for a safe journey to a place where angels will use
his equation to elevate heaven, not to mention
the justice of our last sighs and blessings.

Santos

In Memory of Jose Santos Cox Cheley

One Saturday, in 1991, after a hurricane,
there you were, helping me "clean up"
the wreck of a cottage
I'd just bought after a recession.
You lived across the street
in your wife's adopted mother's house,
owned by a rich younger white woman
she cared for, an absurdity
that somehow made perfect sense.
Suddenly: a new roof, fenced-in yard for my dog,
a studio for my sculptor wife,
and a deck to dream my poems on—yes,
we both agreed, a grown man writing poems
for a living, a hilarious idea.
You dreamed of being an architect,
your wife, Rosy, said, but in Guatemala
one earned callouses, not degrees.
"My Country," you'd say, with sorrow,
as if Guatemala was a place
you'd abandoned and betrayed.
The me you liked wasn't privileged,
educated and assimilated,
but someone who honored memory,
a property you also owned.
For hours we'd watch Penelope catch frisbees,

entranced by the idea of passion
being rewarded by pride. Often
you knew before I did that something
needed to be fixed, replaced, or pardoned,
as if the world of order you esteemed
didn't tolerate the insolence of negligence.
After Rosy died of a heart attack
as you drove her to work at Stop & Shop,
you came by one last time, asking for work.
Crippled by liver disease, too broken to stand,
the money I gave you broke both our hearts.
You once asked why I insisted on going
with you to see a man who refused to pay you.
I didn't really understand why. But I do now.
I wanted to see what your opposite looked like,
someone so lacking in wonder, humor, and elegance.

My Neighbor Ed

I'm getting my watch battery replaced
in our hardware store when I ask Mark,
their watch guy, about my neighbor Ed,
who works here, and whose car I haven't seen
in his driveway in months. "Ed's dead," Mark says,
"he died three months ago, smoking killed him."
Surprised by how aggrieved I am, I stammer
about how Ed lived around the corner from me
on a small side street for over twenty years
and ask why I didn't see an obit anywhere.
Sighing, Mark says, "Well, Ed was grouchy,
and someone has to volunteer to write one."
Yes, he complained if anyone parked near
his tired house, got angry every time my sons
skateboarded down his street, and never once
said hello when I walked my dog past him.
During the pandemic, I tried being nice,
smiling and complimenting his new-old Jeep,
to which he scowled, "It's a vehicle, not a car."
Yes, his sullenness was as familiar as our mailman,
as mysterious as his absence is now. He had a son,
I ask, and Mark says yes but no one here ever saw him,
and Ed never said anything about him. The old woman
with wild white hair always tending his garden,
was she his wife or mother, my wife believed his wife,
I, his mother. "They weren't related, he took care of her
for room and board." When I ask Ed's last name,
Mark is silent a long time, and then, shrugging,

says, "Cobb, I think," which strikes both of us as absurd.
Now I'm wondering, as I wander our village,
why I'm missing someone I didn't know. Am I mourning
the stranger in me, the hidden, secret, unsociable self
who refuses to be agreeable and fears the stranger in others?
Ed, I'm grateful for the light in your kitchen window,
behind the plastic, for the gift of knowing someone lived here,
among the richer, vacant second houses and ominous silence,
enjoying as best you could what remained of your brief
and nameless journey just around the corner from where I live mine.

Ode to The East Hampton Star

Small town village news of births weddings obituaries
plea deals first and last words photos of local life
decoded fumigated and anesthetized: Christmas tree thefts
"revisioning" the (damn) airport land & sea preservation
where (not) to put cellphone towers commit Range Rover rage
one more (or less) loutish shindig celebrating modesty
balloons carpeting the (whole f——) ocean town meetings
hemorrhaging respectability—all those artists' abstract dreams
(appetites) soaked in southwest light splashed all over
God's (private) Garden Party. You know what I mean:
stories articles letters profiles explaining how/why/what
So-and-So said to Never-Will-Be at the Benefit to End Pine Beetles
who's buying spite (wholesale) one Masthead Guestword
Point of (Endless) View at a time. Yes, the plain (godawful) truth
about how (why) the Supervisor of Righteous Outrage (really)
got elected the ex-ex-Mayor quoted Macbeth so much who
(purportedly) donated the Kiwanis' bowling charity the (real) reason
West and East Miller Place no longer speak high school cheating
public housing another parade documenting the history of yesterday
why nobody mourns the (historic) sorrow of windmills.
All that (clanging) enterprise of our settlement makers:
the Millers Bennets Talmages Osbornes Round Swamp Lesters
(Rattrays, most certainly) relishing the dreams of fishermen
farmers and teachers enduring another day hour millennium
of depressions recessions world wars hurricanes and (of course)

pandemics. Yes, our watery phenomenon illuminated editorialized and proofread into a rhapsody of hearsay rumors court orders and D.W.I.s all the way out here at the tip of America's longest island. So okay, yes, let's stand and tip our hats to one more triumphant week (please) of The East Hampton Star, indeed, thank you and Amen!

A Marriage Song

For Edward Hirsch & Lauren Watel

There we all stood, your many friends,
your choir of zealous witnesses,
most strangers until now, enjoying
all the shining pieces of each story
of why you believed fate ordained this day,
Laurie beautiful under a floral crown,
her stories funny and wise, Eddie recounting
the dark miles he traveled to find love,
each a story of spirit, stamina, and grace.
Yes, grace. We each, every one of us,
I believe, understood the odds against,
the expense of such passionate faith.
Yes, in some mysterious, byzantine way
we're all miracles, finally, impossible
and opaque, a luminous blend of chances
we did and didn't take, preambles
we were too frightened to negotiate.
Yes, miracles of light, nonetheless.
Could any of us ever have guessed
how perfectly luminous you both were,
standing there, smiling as you sang
your one song of devotion and rebirth.

Women Rabbis

To Rabbi Debra Stein

At the Big Shul on Rauber Street Grandma argued
with the angels on the purple peeling ceiling about
whether God was a woman. Below, Dad sat with
the other men, worrying about success. Once I asked
Grandma why women weren't rabbis and the blue light
in her eyes shined right through me. Men, she said,
were afraid of women because women knew where
all their dreams were buried, and where to hide
after men blew up the world again. And now,
all these years later, I'm sitting downstairs with men
and women, listening to a woman rabbi welcome
in the New Year, remembering Grandma quoting
from the Talmud: *Be careful if you make a woman cry,
God counts her tears. The Woman came out of a man's rib,
not from his feet to be walked on . . . but from the side
to be equal. And next to the heart to be loved.* Okay,
Grandma's right, things change for the better, and now
if you look up, you'll see her up in the balcony, arguing
about how pleasure and pain, faith and vanity are set
before us like kosher delicacies that we must choose between.
Choose life, Grandma hollers down at me, however bitter
and capricious your misdeeds, humble and exalted
your prayers, history is a mother who alone knows
the recipe for happiness, devotion, and lokshen kugel.

Our Story

For Monica

This morning, while filling your porcelain sculptures
of cakes, cups, and broken dishes with birdseed
for your "girls," as you call your blue jays, cardinals,
and purple finches, you said mostly to yourself,
"I always knew how to learn." Yes, knowledge
is your passion, the reason you studied the Greeks
who esteemed revelation, seduced meaning
out of intuition, sympathy out of bitterness,
who, along with the Hebrews, invented learning,
a story that owns, like us, many names, places,
satisfactions, and other stories, all entwined.
One of which doesn't like to be remembered,
measured, or reasoned with. Yes, I once lived
at ocean's bottom, worshiped only the monarchy
of the self. The story you gave me is a pathway
to the mind and body's fusion, the giving up
of perfection and dancing at ocean's bottom.
A mystery finely honed, perplexing and entwined.
This is why I enjoy watching you make dinner,
holding each essential to the light, as if tasting
its place in our lives, in your large hazel eyes,
a symposium as splendid as any Socrates curated.
Now our story is as mystifying as the wellspring of trust,
the path that leads home. Now before is left behind
and morning begins always for the first time.

For Eli on His Twenty-Fifth Birthday

Yes, I've given you things you didn't ask for,
facets of my DNA that are, well, obsolete
and challenging. Things you've managed
to escape, such as my bellowing at the TV
during political debates. There are qualities
we share, of course, such as empathy for
the downtrodden, who must turn suffering
into imagination. In your laugh your grandfather's
appetite for self-mockery, his passion to turn
the mud of a Russian shtetl into pride and opulence.
In your encyclopedic love of baseball, and
now legal strategy, your mother's passion
for the aesthetics of refinement.

Once I wrote about first hearing of your conception,
how I wandered about in an ecstasy of wonder.
I'm now equally mystified by your curiosity,
by its faith, its buoyancy. How you refit the future
to fit your moment. Once my mother, father, and I
trudged across empty housing lots looking for a life
we never found. Now your room at home still guards
your dreams, on this, the longest day of light
when the sun's reach exceeds all expectation.

What Comes Next

For Augie on His Twenty-Second Birthday

Last Saturday, we enjoyed one of our talks,
in which we discuss something troubling you
from every possible perspective. You were five
when they began, your eyes bright in your child seat,
as we discussed why your kindergarten teacher,
Mrs. Mathews, called you August, and not Augie.
Who was this August, you wanted to know,
surely not someone who loved sports the way you did,
who enjoyed belonging to a team committed
to the same ideal? Augie was who you liked being,
the kind of boy you wanted as a friend, even teachers
can't know everything, we decided. Every Saturday
we'd drive out to Cedar Point to watch the geese,
analyzing all your feelings about the world you were learning
one revelation at a time. Too often, your older brother, Eli,
was the subject. I tried to explain that as an only child
I envied you having these problems, the intimacy
of overlapping natures and boundaries. And once
you asked why I wrote something nobody understood.
We both found my garbled answer hilarious.
This Saturday we walked a beach in Montauk, watching
your surfer friends spool their signatures along the horizon,
discussing a subject as perplexing as any: your future.
You know what you don't want: to sit alone in a room,
seeking inspiration, as your sculptor mother and I do.

Yes, you're familiar with the benefits of satisfaction,
but require the company of other human beings, not ideas,
however illuminating. As always, I enjoyed our talk
but perhaps failed to say that I understand better now
the difference between being an Augie and August.
It's passion you want, not a title or career, an idea you can join,
perfect, and struggle against. Yes, it's frightening, what comes next,
and, as you drove us home, lost in thought, there you were again,
the torpedo baby, hurtling himself over his crib, impatient
for new phenomena to begin, one silvered curlicued wave at a time.

Penelope

A Border Collie mix with amber eyes, black,
white and blue merle coat, my other wife,
my wife called her, a work dog, her job,
she said, was to keep me company,
and Penelope seemed to take this to mean
never leaving me alone. Clearly the man
she loved was smarter, handsomer, better
than me. A delusion we both enjoyed.
All those mornings lying at my feet, listening
to every word I wrote, even those about her,
never complaining or leaving the room.
She was my reason to take a break, or go walking
along the ocean and woods. Once, coming back
from an errand when I couldn't bring her,
I found our mailman, furnace and UPS guys
herded in our yard, waiting to be set free,
while she, in the grass, off to the side, lay
watching them. Always a step or two ahead,
she helped raised our sons, who now, along
with my wife, want another dog, less fierce,
with a lower IQ. Yes, I understand, but,
like her namesake, who every night undid
every stitch to delay remarrying and wait
for her true love, Odysseus, such devotion is rare,
and, in my case, equally deluded, and unconditional.

The Designer

A Birthday Prayer for Jack Ceglic

Bless the perfect sheen of your high white walls
the lilting cadence of your towering glass windows
filling your mornings with light

all your happy kitchens
and gleaming stoves
simmering with scents of paradise

the litanies your houses sing
to their roofs and cellars
elegant as the wings of swallows

bless your pure and generous heart
the arias your day lilies sing to Manuel
the architect of your dreams

bless the faces you have painted
with prophetic imagination
their eyes spiced with garlic and chives

bless the love you've given to us
your eternal neighbors
the design you turned into our home

bless your elegant wings
that have lifted us higher
than we believed we could go.

The Middle

Squeezed between the above
and the below, the furthermore
and the never mind, the middle
was always climbing up
and down itself, trying to expand
and disappear, surprised
by its own hunger, and rage,
its ideas as peculiar as the
countries it left behind.
Those of us who lived below
aspired to its better schools
and neighborhoods, believing
it was where God lived one day
a week, and nobody was hated
by everyone else. After all,
looking up is better than
looking down. Basically,
we believed the middle
was a vast backyard without
checkpoints, passports
and wars, just lush gardens
and bright birds singing
about trust and fidelity
to everything left behind.
Basically, we were what
was left behind. Happiness,
our black-and-white TV said,
was owning your own house

and car, syntax, and God,
never feeling abased or spent.
Essentially, it was wanting
what you believed you would
never have, the other side of
everything you didn't understand,
darkness smothered in light,
names you could pronounce
without an accent, just once.

Early and Late

Early wants everything in its place,
likes worrying about things,
especially being late,
which is why it can't stop shaking your hand
and avoiding your eyes.
Late wants nothing to do with superstition or style,
will never under any circumstance apologize.
Early enjoys being interrupted, overlooked,
and decisively misunderstood.
Late fears only not being late enough
to be seen as ascendingly weird.
Both believe only in riddles, paradoxes,
and the rewards of being impervious and cursed.
Neither care for what Buddhism calls "the seat of truth,"
or any other kind of vain contentment.
As for myself, I believe it best to be sudden,
all at once, and somewhat invisible,
in never standing too close or far away from myself,
being too early or late to accept my fate,
because, essentially, only the dead
don't care what others think,
which is why I try never to go anywhere,
seldom speak
and would dare to write
anything this inane.

My Mistakes

Human life must be some kind of mistake.
—ARTHUR SCHOPENHAUER

My mistakes like to argue about which is the most offensive,
their importance in our shared hierarchy
of unforgivable deficiencies. Each, apparently,
desires to be the most abhorrent and reviled.
Simple ones, the things I shouldn't have said or done,
words and names I mispronounced,
friends I insulted without knowing why,
get pushed aside by the more spirited ones.
One especially enjoys reminding me
what I said during a radio interview
about a poet I thought I admired
that was so envious and spiteful
the radio host, looking for controversy,
wouldn't let me change the subject.
Sure, this one mistake whispers in the shower,
it hurt many feelings, but I didn't have
to accommodate him so keenly.
One waits until I'm asleep to ask why,
after all my father poems, in my one mother poem,
after all her sacrifices, I mentioned her bunions
and weak ankles, which hurt her so deeply?
This one surely stands out, it likes to shout!
Some are satisfied with simply stripping me
of any lingering confidence but others enjoy

continuing ignobility. Yes, I try to ignore them,
focus on more practical matters, like bill-paying
and walking my dog Binx along the ocean,
but even then, there they are, hobbling behind,
sulking and bickering about which did the most harm,
is the cruder and more intrusive. It's no use reminding them
who provides a home, they know my passion for self-loathing
is irresistible, one treasured mispronunciation at a time.

Blame

> *Woe to us, for the wrath of God has come*
> *upon . . . that we*
> *should congregate with the dead . . . like an*
> *unloved wife . . .*
> —THE DEAD SEA SCROLLS

This morning a four-month-old boy
was found wrapped in plastic
at the bottom of a 33-foot well.
Born to addicted parents,
a foster mother attempted
unconditional love but, due
to a technicality, the state
returned him to his parents.
The newspaper listed several conditions
for blame: the welfare office neglected
supervision, the court system, overcome
by its inventory of the hopeless,
failed to recognize its responsibilities.
At four months, the human brain owns
enough consciousness to recognize harm,
its deprivations. Cioran, the Romanian thinker,
believed consciousness a disease.
With its endless U-turns, dead ends
and detours, consciousness
can be performed anywhere,
even at the bottom of a well.

My wife's mother survived four years
in a Siberian labor camp, where,
to persevere and render horror
mundane, her sensitivity and perception
were sealed in plastic. As we speak,
Ukraine is being expunged,
swallowed whole by a tyrant
addicted to self-aggrandizement,
zealous and irrational ignominy. Yes,
all our endless, peculiar, if glorious, failings
in only the first chapter of Genesis,
the pursuit of such diverse posterity!
Hobbes said, *"if he had read as much as other men,*
he should have been as ignorant as they."
Indeed, our appetite for suffering
is implacable in its devotion to detail,
pitiless in its affinity for slander and bewilderment.
Horror uses one performance to distract us
from another. Refrain from reason, a machine
like any other, blame can be performed anywhere,
on balconies and deep in the cornices of rage and sorrow,
with and without benevolence, only apathy is required.
If you must find blame, blame yourself for seeking refuge in words.

My Heart

My heart loves the paintings and books I love long before I do,
swears unending loyalty and faith
even if I often don't know
the difference between
what I want and need to believe.
Yes, like all vital foundations,
it can be a hornet's nest
of duty and provocation,
the tyranny of all things elusive and nuanced.
Which is why perhaps,
knowing it'll be despised,
it will wake me in the middle of the night
to tell me a truth it knows
I'll at least try to turn into a poem
about something
we both desperately
want me to finally understand.
Such as: why, in a dark time,
it's a source of such great wonder and strength,
oriented toward the good,
a prophet, let's say,
forever suffering,
in its devotion to me,
incurable melancholy and blindness,
a kind of Job forever worrying

about being inspired enough
to flourish *like a flower*
and then *inevitably*
be cut down
and given away.

Democracy

> *A charming form of government, full of variety
> and disorder,
> dispensing a sort of equality to equals and
> unequals alike.*
>
> —PLATO

On this cold November evening,
democracy and I are walking along the ocean,
arguing about why everyone in my old neighborhood
hated where everyone else came from,
behaved as if hate was our faith,
envy and prejudice, our nature.
Sometimes, after arguing,
democracy and I reminisce
about a past we both believe
loved us more than it does now.
But not tonight, tonight, feeling vulnerable,
it admits, it can be clumsy, even suspicious,
occasionally cruel and overbearing,
but remember, it hums, George Washington
and Abe Lincoln thought I was worth dying for,
Plato believed my soul is immortal,
and therefore indestructible.
Yes, I cry, but he also saw you as the tyranny
of the ignorant majority, a collision
of the just and the jaundiced,
the frenzy of the marketplace,

preferred an aristocracy of philosopher-kings.
Still, we agree, a splendid idea
about passion, reason, and change,
protecting oneself against one's ignorance and greed,
the technicolor kingdom our dreams live in.
Yes, democracy and I lament,
here we are, again, at war
with the delirious and self-obsessed,
teetering on a precipice, singing a song
half-swallowed and off-key,
about our hunger for satisfaction,
the intrinsic goodness that feeds
our inmost being, yes, here we are,
riddles wrapped in a theory hidden
in a paradox about the mind's hunger
for something as redolent and willfully
unremitting as dignity, as hopeful
and curiously radical as happiness,
and yes, as tormented and ever-fleeting,
as magnificently surprising and pleasing
in its reach as, yes, say it—freedom!

Something and Nothing

ONE

The world is driven by blind dissatisfied will seeking satisfaction, the cause, purpose, and essence of something.
—ARTHUR SCHOPENHAUER

1

In our attic on Maria Street, buried
under boxes of Uncle Jake's girly magazines,
a first edition of Schopenhauer's essays
spoke to me of suffering and strife,
the vanities of the outer and inner man,
and the martyrdom of "almost all those
who truly enlighten humanity."
Yes, our hunger for what lives in us
just out of reach, his framework,
splintered scaffolding for understanding
our restless pursuit of satisfaction,
the something that can only be attained
through the genius of thinking
that stains civilization
only occasionally
with benevolence.

Yes, the madness, the failure,
the nothing Dad bequeathed us,

that talked to us in our sleep, believed
only in the heretical, imperious fate
that took us back to Grandma's house
deep in the shrunken inner city, where all
the disgraced languages lived on porches
with falling roofs, arguing
whose desperation presented
the most lasting gifts, yes, the fate
that took Mom back to her old filing job,
to watch the same big clock hand
crawl around the same smaller one
until it was time to take the No. 4 bus back
to the blueberry ice cream she ate out of the icebox
late at night to forget her boss calling her
Lil' Something
and everyone laughing.

Yes, the ravenous fate
that dragged us back to the gurgling junkyard sinks,
toilets and rampaging rats lurking
just beyond our backyard fence,
the stink Mom and I were born in,
that Dad promised to rescue her from before
fate snatched his accountant's name,
embezzling everything he owned
one week before their wedding,
and then moved him into her mother's house
for "just until I get back on my feet,"
where he stayed for twenty years.

2

Yes, the same opaque,
petulant fate that returned me
to the stained-glass gloom of the attic,
to Uncle Jake's moldy boxes of girly books,
where the ever-angry god of shame
thanked fate repeatedly, and then pointed
down the hall to Jake's other buried army
of boxers, knaves, and fairy queens
feigning sleep in the first editions of Hemingway,
T. S. Eliot, Ezra Pound, and dear Mr. Yeats,
whose widening gyres, singing nightingales
and "half-savage" Mr. Mauberley I pillaged
when Jake left to open his technicolor kingdom
of dreams from his perch high behind
the Paramount's CinemaScope screen
on John Wayne, Humphrey Bogart, and Donald Duck,
yes, the enlightenment, the martyrdom,
the largess Schopenhauer promised.

The same spiteful, persnickety fate
that many years later, in the library
of the writing retreat where I wasn't writing,
opened a volume of modern paintings
to the molten, ochre faces, unfingered hands
and possessed eyes of a flower-clutching boy
and his mother floating in spectral abstraction,
yes, the sentience, the hieroglyphic splendor
of Arshile Gorky's *The Artist and His Mother*
which suddenly was speaking to me

in the voice of a librarian asking
if I wanted to borrow the book
I was so taken with, it was closing time.

Yes, the dark anathema, the want,
the pain in their eyes, peering out
of the butchery of the death march
of the Armenian Genocide designed
to kill every man, woman and child,
that Gorky, his sister Vartoosh, their
mother Shushan, and two half-sisters,
survived, when, to feed them, this mother
starved herself, dying seven years later
of starvation in her son's arms, yes,
the delirium, the seething that greeted us
on every porch, front yard, and angry
sullen garden in our old neighborhood,
the ungodly wars and holocaust obliterations
these evacuee neighbors refused to survive,
that lay festering inside their tiny, worried houses,
frightened porches, the same grudging beliefs
arguing in Czech, Ukrainian, Irish, German,
Italian and Yiddish about who belonged here more,
came before anyone else, could invent the best
American persona and alibi, and, finally,
understood what being here really meant,
as if knowing meant owning the will to achieve
something greater than the gangrenous dread
that now scalded Mom's blue eyes when she opened
Grandma's front door and walked back inside.

3

In the new backyard snow this morning,
in the sycamores leaning ever closer,
in the big walloping ocean wind
and high morning sky, unfolding ever so gently,
in the smell of coffee downstairs,
in the hands of my wife, making it,
the simmering deliverance, the unbridled light
we, wearing masks, after months of lockdown,
sought on my birthday, January 6, 2021,
in our local museum's sculpture garden,
where, from the hazardous assemblage of apes,
parrots, Venuses, and that liar of liars,
Mr. Pinocchio himself, all spread over
a tractor's ruthless rake, the cavernous eyes
of death's giant skull glared at us out of
the savage paradox of art's insurrection
in Jim Dine's *The Wheatfield (Agincourt)*,
when, suddenly, our phones began wailing
with an even more prolix assemblage,
an even more savage kind of insurrection,
which now was attacking our Capitol
because Pinocchio himself told it to,
yes, now we too were staring out of death's
cavernous eyes into the raging inferno Jim Dine,
Arshile Gorky, and Pinocchio himself personified.

4

All truth passes through three stages:
First, it is ridiculed; second, it is violently opposed;
and third, it is accepted as self-evident.
—ARTHUR SCHOPENHAUER

Now, aimless, ancient, and perplexed,
my wife and I, fearing being swallowed up
by the barbarity of every wrong turn,
dead end and vulgar cul-de-sac fate
had so brazenly assembled for us,
yes, we were fleeing, I believed, the furor
and stagnation entrenched in the eyes
of the boy and his mother in Gorky's painting,
the symphony of who me?, never again, and same to you,
performed every Saturday night in corner bars
in my old neighborhood by the woebegone
for whom hate is the most cohesive union,
yes, the permission to be primitive out loud
that Mr. Pinocchio himself was giving to
his rollicking hoard of primitives to attack
the very thing they believed was being
taken away from them, yes, the question Pascal,
that 17th century mathematical genius, asked:
were we each an "incomprehensible monster,"
byzantine, willful, and unhappy enough
to "humble the exalted and exalt the humbled,"
to begin to accept as self-evident

the very thing Pinocchio was attacking,
in other words, were we worthy of
so beautiful, prescient, and brittle
an idea as democracy?

5

Yes, it's Sunday morning and Mom, Dad,
and me are slathering buttery waffles
with vanilla ice cream at our favorite
hot dog joint on Lake Ontario, happy
to be away from Maria Street, when,
yes, once again, irascible fate introduces
the unimaginable so nonchalantly
I don't know why I'm suddenly mocking
the way Mom is loudly smacking her lips
and sighing while smiling at me, yes, smiling
as if I'm the reason waffles taste so good,
anything is delicious, no, being nine years old
and owning someone else's happiness isn't easy,
the only one she ever tells all her stories to,
how three of her teachers came to plead
with her orthodox father not to take her
out of school in the tenth grade, she's brilliant,
writes beautifully, please, Mr. Bernstein,
let her mind learn to speak, become special,
she's too young to go to work, how all her friends
escaped Maria Street, live in their own homes
in nicer neighborhoods, don't have to pretend
to be less unhappy, while Dad tells everyone

we live in the suburbs, in a split-level house
with a silver pool in the backyard and a bowling alley
in the basement, why, nevertheless, she dresses me
in clothes she can't afford, claps when I enter a room,
yes, love is expensive, owns even our dreams,
she says, is this why she's sighing so profoundly
she doesn't notice Dad's lips silently moving
in the booth right beside her, yes, once again
he's talking to the only person he enjoys talking to,
himself, probably telling off a factory boss that stores
his vending machines, remembering everything
he didn't say when it mattered, and now she's crying
as she picks up a catchup bottle and, pointing it at me,
closes her eyes and squeezes it with all the strength
in her two small hands, which is why I'm ducking
as a big red spray goes whooshing over my head
to hit the man, his wife and three kids in the booth
behind us, all dressed in their Sunday best, why
suddenly the whole world is staring at us
out of such big blotched gaudy red eyes.

TWO

Esau said to his father, "Do you have only one blessing, my father? Bless me too, my father!" Then Esau wept aloud.
—GENESIS 27

1

Recently, asked by the Favorite Poem Project
to pick a Bible story and explain why,
I immediately picked the story of Jacob
tricking his brother Esau out of his birthright
and then their father's blessing,
and knew why. Yes, it's a story about greed,
betrayal, and shameful pride, about why
Esau was said to despise his birthright.
I know because I also despise mine.
In the depths of my being my older sister Phyllis
lives in me like an echo, a suspicion,
and an unborn soul. After Phyllis was stillborn,
Mom was told not to give birth again,
it was too dangerous, but she wanted me,
Grandma said, more than her life.
What Grandma didn't say is what we both believed:
that I'd stolen my sister Phyllis's life.
Which is why I've always suspected my desires,
strove after the impossible, risked my life
on whims, and hid inside nameless shadows,
why Mom told everyone I wasn't an only child,
Dad sometimes couldn't remember my name

or how old I was, why my imaginary friends
almost never survived their dangerous missions,
and my guardian angel was a peacock with
iridescent feathers, why so often I pretend
to be someone less obsessed with echoes
and suspicions, who doesn't believe
all his blessings are stillborn,
and despised.

2

Yes, birthrights, blessings, and birthdays,
intermingling, blurring, and fleeing one another,
as the future itself fled Pinocchio's wrath
on my birthday, January 6, 2021,
and was being squeezed out of me
on my eighth birthday by two powerful
Lithuanian women, Mom and Grandma,
all of us sitting fully clothed in a bathtub,
a chair lodged against the door, praying
for Dad and Uncle Jake to come home
and save us from the banging on our windows
and doors by our six worst Russian neighbors,
who believed themselves entitled to the vile privileges
fate alone ordained, all now shouting, "Filthy Jew demons!"
Yes, the same hate that consumed the Armenians
and tortured Vostanig's mother and was placing me
now between Mom and Grandma in an empty bathtub,
that believed hate didn't require a soul or sympathy,
only blind allegiance and rage, yes, rage, and therefore

was easier to obey than something that required,
essentially, faith, yes, faith, the same nothing
and hate Dad's father fled, that selected the heads
of wives, brothers, and mothers the Cossacks hung
on their doors, that imprisoned my wife's mother
in a labor camp in Soviet Uzbekistan, and then
ordered her mother and what remained of her family
who returned to their Polish town after the war
to get back on their train or be killed by those
now living in their house, yes, the same nothing
and hate wearing Nazi, Home Guard, and neighbors'
faces that boarded their train at every stop to rob
and shoot Jews in the fields outside their window,
yes, please, imagine my wife's fifteen-year-old mother
and uncle struggling not to look Jewish-enough
to be murdered hour after hour, stop after stop
until Sweden finally found them on a map
somewhere north of Hell.

Yes, please imagine the three of us clutching
one another in a bathtub, all of us pleading
with fate to have mercy on us, while, above,
a flock of geese flapped across our tiny roof window
like angels of mercy promising to deliver us
from those who despised our birthright
for reasons none of us understood, all of us praying
at the top of our humble and exalted voices
for God to please please please have pity on us . . .

3

On June 15, 1915, Shushan and her children (Gorky, Vartoosh, and their two half-sisters), like nearly all Armenians who weren't slaughtered outright, were put on deportation marches that were like walking concentration camps, where men were tortured and shot, women and girls raped and killed, and children abducted and murdered . . .

—PETER BALAKIAN, "ARSHILE GORKY: FROM THE ARMENIAN GENOCIDE TO THE AVANT-GARDE"

After fate abandoned Vostanig along with his mother
and sisters to their neighbors, the Turks, Kurds,
Mussulmans and Cossack-inspired Hamidiye,
all of whom did their best to annihilate
what remained of the Armenians, because,
essentially, they dared to be Christian and exist
outside their primitive jurisdictions, yes,
long after their orphans were attacked,
their houses burned down, horseshoes
and wild animals were nailed to their feet
and backs, after fate starved Vostanig's
adored mother, Shushan, of her essence
and murdered his sister, Sima, it changed
Vostanig Adoian's name to Arshile Gorky,
after his hero, Maxim, so everyone would think
him Russian, not Armenian, and therefore
less despised, Gorky found the essential will
to shove fate aside, and make his great paintings,

*The Liver is the Cock's Comb, How My Mother's
Embroidered Apron Unfolds* and, finally, *Agony*,
yes, after Gorky reclaimed Vostanig and Shushan
from the inferno of time, fate designed his end
by first burning his studio down, then stealing
his family and injuring his spine, yes, after
the 46-year-old Gorky could no longer find
the fervor, the alchemy, the genius that turned
paint into flesh and blood, the restless hunger
that sustained him through famine, torture,
and endless degradation, yes, after all the genius
was gone, he stood before a blank canvas,
pondering the remedy fate proposed to end
his remembering being eight years old
and posing with Shushan for the photo from
which *The Artist and His Mother* was created,
yes, after the ten years of the pain and agony
of imagining revelation and transcendence,
he said goodbye to the color and shape of Shushan
and hanged himself.

4

Yes, who better than Schopenhauer himself
could understand why belittled and angry fate
would wander lost through the labyrinth of time,
amidst its own satisfactions, yes, the very satisfactions
believed by Schopenhauer to be nothing less
than the "supreme object of life," only to place,
for a reason perhaps only something understood,

Schopenhauer himself, stooped, disheveled,
and preoccupied at the foot of my bed,
scratching his mutton chops, yes,
Schopenhauer was visiting a dream
fate itself had selected for me, yawning forlornly,
as if he too was now wondering why
in this world of endless suffering
I was so obsessed with my understanding
of his most peculiar, brutal idea, yes,
the seeking of the joy that arrives uninvited
at a festival in which Nothing is a tuxedoed MC,
ordering everyone around, while Something sits
at the back of the room, feeling overlooked.
"But, Professor," I cry, "you yourself are uninvited
and isn't that something?" Laughing, he says,
"Yes, but why would you believe any of my ideas
would want anything to do with you?"
Flummoxed, I can think of only one thing to ask:
"What is the reason for my obsession
with Gorky's obsession with his mother—is it all
about sacrifice, striving after something always
out of reach, the 'manifold restless motion . . .
of hunger and sexual instinct,' of something
being rewarded with only nothing?" Seeing that I
understand little of all this, he, swallowing
another yawn, says, "Dear child, blame if you must
superfluous and demented fate, but fate rewards
only our illusions, the monster in us is but a test of will,
ask instead only what the nature of something and nothing
is struggling so vehemently to save you from,
yes, what it is you're asking of yourself?"

Then, in a whuff, he's gone, without an answer,
leaving only the memory of a festival in which,
for a moment, joy arrives uninvited,
and sacrifice is a test of will fate itself fears.

5

Yes, here I am, ensconced in another dream
fate has selected for me, this time I'm adrift
in Gorky's studio barn, intruding on a photo
of him working on *The Artist and His Mother*,
both of us now surrounded by shameless color
jumping over and under memory holding hands
with wistfulness, each worshiping only itself,
and over there, in the far corner of his fixation,
the hard and brittle queen, mortality, conferring
with her sacred friend, sacrifice, all spread over
palpitating canvas, and there, to the far right,
look and see virtue confiding in vanity, vanity
in deceit, everywhere the willful obstructs
the boorish, truth dancing with damaged pride,
yes, color magnifying and projecting itself on
what remains of the genius of wonder, which,
despite slaughter, starvation, and every kind
of cruelty, endures, yes, the genius of wonder
continues somehow to realize, deny, apotheosize,
and think with and without a why, yes, continues
to refuse to disown even one puny therefore
or because like the bright Saturday afternoon
when Dad finally made a business successful

enough to move us out of Grandma's house
into a basement apartment just over the city line,
renting not owning but now Mom owns two bedrooms,
one bath, three closets and a kitchenette
big enough for three, certainly me, sixteen,
refusing to sit all scrunched up between two oldsters,
but hey, look! Mom's smile is running around
opening and shutting closets and toilet doors,
yes, everything is lifted out of a department store window,
a U-shaped sofa big enough to surround a breakfront
full of glistening new dishes in a real breathing living room,
which is why Mom's hands can't stop touching themselves
and Dad is hopping around measuring how high
wide deep everything is, his eyes selling something
to nothing, selling why to maybe and if only possible,
while I'm deep inside my new bedroom, making sure
the door locks, the bed and floor don't creak, yes,
space inside of which I'll put my easel and paints,
soon start a new high school wearing new smiles,
maybe even get a car, no, it's not a split-level house
with a bowling alley in the basement but look,
there's a pool in the center of this apartment complex
(where Dad will put a soda machine), yes,
never has fate promised so much something
without a niggling nothing, no, never this kind of light
dancing in Mom's blue eyes, so much supreme
sweet something streaming through every
new shining sunlit window!

THREE

Today I painted so intensely that my knees are trembling . . . The agonies and torments in my mind impel me to recognize that I must have been born to suffer for art . . .
—FROM GORKY'S LETTER TO HIS SISTER, APRIL 18, 1938, IN NOURITZA MATOSSIAN, *BLACK ANGEL: A LIFE OF ARSHILE GORKY*

1

Yes, all those thugs fate made wait outside
our school to charge the Jewish kids lunch money
to go inside, and no, I wouldn't because Dad
wouldn't and I didn't want him to know I did,
which is why I had to fight one or two or three
bigger ones in the playground after school,
and sometimes fate provided a Saturday morning
cartoon festival to hide inside maybe because
neither of us could pronounce any of those slippery
sour syllables or swallow their dictionaries full
of insatiable definitions, and both had to repeat
third grade after repeating first and eat lunch
at a diner to avoid ridicule in the school cafeteria,
yes, fate and me, sitting next to all the solemn men
from Kodak, Bonds and DuPont, staring out
dirty windows into the frozen future, both of us
playing hooky skipping stones over the icy Genesee River,
fleeing the fraught music of our minds' broken keyboard,

neither of us knowing our right hand from our left,
why one sentence clause dominated another,
yes, we both believed failure and stupidity
were our legacy, slept bunched together on
a wobbly pullout sofa listening to the rats dancing
the kazatsky on our roof like drunken Cossacks
because, yes, even though only fate knew it then,
we were both dyslexic, wandering together
down shame's dark corridors, Mom insisting the taunts,
mimicry and injured pride were our advantage,
the same off-key garbled lullabies fate crooned
in our ears late at night, the same tortured impetus
Gorky turned into color to quiet all the Hamidiye screeching,
all of us, Gorky, fate, the rats, and me dancing
ever more desperately over the broken roofs
of our minds like, yes, drunken Cossacks.

2

Yes, here I am, all grown up and alone on my porch,
bald, with a small belly, eating chocolate ice cream
while looking up at the tantalizing anonymity
of the ancient, feckless stars, feeling besmirched
and stealthy, all wrapped up inside an illusion
wrapped inside a half-truth, me, fate and reality,
maybe existence, too, all of us seeking a mother,
maybe because, as Schopenhauer said, "misfortune
in general is the rule," yes, all of us are seeking
the origins of our originality, the cathedral of dreams

that transforms wonder into transcendence,
the nothing out of which something is made,
yes, all our precious forms of certainty forever asking
why we play such minor roles in our own dreams,
yes, what Plato called *continual Becoming and never Being*,
the reason Pinocchio gave sabotage and calumny fists
and legs to kick and tear asunder our most original idea,
why he empowered his philistines to disembowel truth
and honor, render the righteous helpless because
sometimes something gets stuck in nothing
and can't free itself, yes, please, look up and see him
sitting high on his golden throne of saturated greed,
engorged and gloating, instigating the end-of-time spectacle
of violence, yes, our most sacred beliefs enslaved
and forced to pray to the god of savagery, who wants
everyone on their knees unable to remember why
only yesterday every field burned with meaning,
every blessing a snow crystal one could shake and shake
until deep in the whirlpool of our being truth and honor
rejoice, yes, rejoice in the splendor of unconditional freedom.

3

Fate seldom bothers to phone anymore,
prefers to hear its declarations bounce
around my dreams, but occasionally a deputy
delivers bad news. No drums, marching bands,
or whispers, just a quiet ringing from Mom's
best friend, Bea, who lives two floors below
in the state-run assisted living complex

where Mom has enjoyed no Jake or angry languages,
just the ever-savory tang of sovereignty,
but now Bea has called to let me know Mom
keeps misplacing things, can't remember
where Sunday put Monday, who took
her wedding ring, yes, she sobs, it's time
I came and did something, something
is called for, only this morning
she lost her last favorite photo of me.
Now I'm in an airplane flying alongside
all the sorrow-stuffed clouds fate is using
to spell out the word *stowaway* as a reminder
of my place in Schopenhauer's "realm of *finality*,"
yes, fate is bouncing me on shame's squeaky knee,
because, yes, I waited too long to marry,
give Mom a bride and infant, why,
after so much sacrifice and disappointment,
Mom's mind now dreams in hieroglyphs,
belongs to the god of perplexity, which is why
I'm now a stranger trying to explain why
she's moving into a facility with full-time doctors
and nurses, yes, an Alzheimer's ward,
where memory is sought after and treasured,
rides a merry-go-round of plaque-coated neurons,
meanders between childhood and last week,
yes, she knows the name of the boy, Isadore,
who took her to her first dance and the milkman
who sang the tenor aria from *La Bohème*
while delivering sour cream, but not where
the recent past is hiding, it seems to have disappeared,
yes, it's my fault Mom doesn't know the infant

I'm holding is her grandson, that even fate doesn't know
why Mom is smiling past me at nothing,
why nothing has taken my mother away,
turned time into a mirror in which loneliness
owns a thousand faces.

4

Yes, the three of us, Mom, Dad and me, deep
in the lush dark of the living room, watching
on our tiny black-and-white TV the endless parade
of beautiful people dancing up and down stairs,
along runways, stepping famously out of limousines,
everyone, especially Mom and me, congratulating
success on being successful, yes, success the name
the theme the reason for this annual jamboree,
the Academy Awards, for which Mom puts on
such bright red lipstick, her best shiny blue dress
with fake silver buttons and pearl earrings,
sits so straight up on one of Jake's red kitchen chairs,
whispering thanks to the ceiling for allowing
such a splendorous panorama to take place
in our living room, on Maria Street, where
few miracles ever happen, and there's Dad
leaning back against the toilet door, imitating
all those "hugging and kissing phonies,"
hugging and kissing only himself, and way over there,
in the dining room, Grandma is sleeping
sitting up on her pull-out sofa, dreaming
of Lithuanian weddings, yes, all of us hiding

within these three tiny hours of annual sanctum
in which neither the scarcity of nothing
nor forever looming Uncle Jake exist.

And then, every year, this night ends
and Dad turns off the TV and carries me off to bed
where Mom sings her lullabies about our longing
for ever more something, and yes, there she is,
Mom, smiling brilliantly, because she knows
how beautiful I think she is, even if or despite
the fact that Schopenhauer said none of us
are ever happy, we're always striving after something
hiding in Mom's endless washing, ironing and filing
of other people's more important papers, in the coins
she counts and stacks into gleaming towers,
in her believing only in me, for this one shiny night,
us, mother and son, adorned in gleaming tribute,
striving for something just beyond our reach.

5

Yes, suddenly, floating in unrelenting wonder,
not the black and white of the Gorky photo,
or all those photos of Mom and me bathed in adulation,
but another mother and son photo, yes,
my wife, Monica, and our newborn son, Eli,
curled deep in her arms, his puffy red eyes opening
after their long night of pushing against the immeasurable,
yes, he's smiling, as if he already knows that in each
knurled breath of his newborn imagination,

in each precious cry there's something larger finer
more exquisite than all his worries and fears,
that now the smiling man holding him up to the light
is me, his father, yes, that after all my fretful zigzags
praying at the altar of extravagance,
the scared boy hiding in the man
has finally gathered in all the estranged pieces
of his now ever-expanding story
into this one precious newborn moment,
and there, in Monica's large hazel eyes,
time itself is whirling
and singing dance dance dance
for all you're worth
which is something and nothing
and, yes, everything in between.

ACKNOWLEDGMENTS

I am grateful to the editors of these magazines, books, and newspapers in which many of these poems first appeared: *Epiphany*, *Five Points*, *Literary Matters*, *The East Hampton Star*, *The First Fifty Years: A Jubilee in Prose and Poetry Honoring Women Rabbis*, the *Gettysburg Review*, *Salmagundi*, the *Southern Review*, the *Threepenny Review*, and the *Yale Review*.

I drew inspiration and invaluable information from Peter Balakian's *Vise and Shadow: Essays on the Lyric Imagination, Poetry, Art, and Culture*, and an essential quote from his important essay, "Arshile Gorky: From the Armenian Genocide to the Avant-Garde." I also drew inspiration and a quote from Nouritza Matossian's *Black Angel: A Life of Arshile Gorky*.

Lasting gratitude to friends who read these poems in their various incarnations: Carl Dennis, Drenka Willen, Robert Pinsky, Edward Hirsch, Grace Schulman, Marc Frons, Georges Borchardt, my wife, Monica Banks, and especially my editor, Jill Bialosky.